CATCH IT!

Contents

Diana Bentley

Story illustrated by
Pet Gotohda

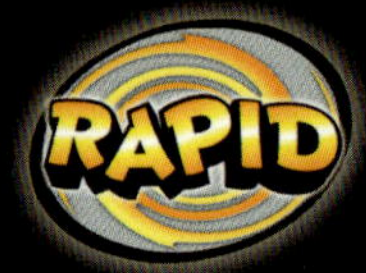

Find out about

- Different breeds of watch dogs

Tricky words

- watch
- loud
- intruders
- sharp
- eyes

Text starter

Lots of dogs make good watch dogs. They have sharp eyes and sharp hearing. If they see or hear an intruder, they bark loudly.

Watch Dogs
Lots of dogs make
good watch dogs.

This small dog has a loud bark.
It can watch out for intruders.

This dog makes a good
watch dog.

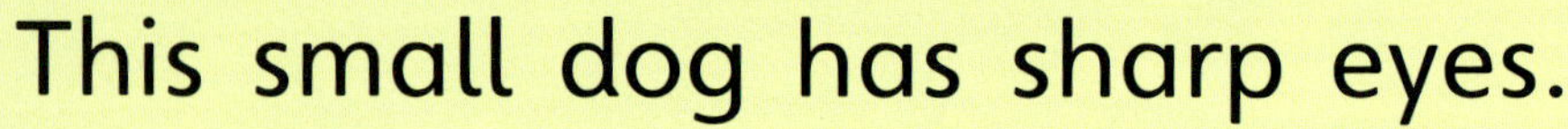

This small dog has sharp eyes.

It can watch out for intruders.

This dog makes a good watch dog.

This big dog has a loud bark.

It can watch out for intruders.

This dog makes a good
watch dog.

10

Text Detective

- What kinds of dog make good watch dogs?
- Why can small dogs make good watch dogs?

Word Detective

- **Phonic Focus:** Final phonemes

  Page 4: Find a word that ends with the phoneme 'll'.
- Page 8: Find the adjective that describes the dog's bark.
- Page 10: Find a small word inside the word 'good'.

Super Speller

Read these words:

can   has

Now try to spell them!

HA! HA! HA!

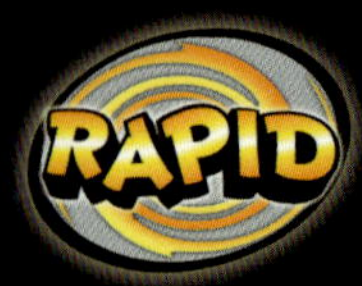

In this story

 Bones

 The master

 Wag

 The burglar

 The postman

Tricky words

- burglar
- garden
- barked
- postman

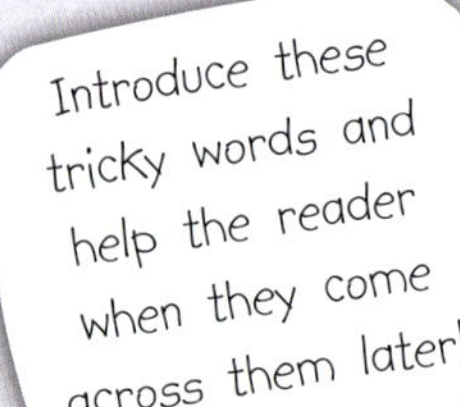

Story starter

Bones is a big dog. Wag is a small dog. Bones is a very good dog but Wag is always getting into trouble. One day, Bones saw a burglar coming into the garden.

The Burglar

Bones saw a burglar
in the garden.

Bones ran at the burglar.
He barked and barked.

The burglar ran off.

The master saw the burglar.
"Good dog, Bones,"
said the master.

The master gave Bones
a bone.

Wag saw the postman in the garden.

Wag ran at the postman.
He barked and barked.

"Help! Help!"
said the postman.

The master saw the postman
in the garden.

"Stop! Stop!" said the master. "Get off, Wag!"

"Bad dog, Wag,"
said the master.

Quiz

Text Detective

- Why did Wag attack the postman?
- What do you think the master will say to the postman after Wag's attack?

Word Detective

- **Phonic Focus:** Final phonemes

  Page 15: Find a word ending with the phoneme 'ff'.
- Page 18: What two words make the word 'postman'?
- Page 22: Find the word 'stop' twice.

Super Speller

Read these words:

big   man

Now try to spell them!

HA! HA! HA!

Q What did the dog say to the burglar?

A "Stop in the name of the paw!"

24